Letters to My Former Self

Temote Matsu

You traveled all this way in hopes of a life of adventure. You left home, family, and friends with the intent of finding meaning and purpose. You want to mimic that which you read in books and see in movies. But it was not here, at least not in the way you had imagined.

Book I

Hard Truths

LETTER I

Stop feeling sorry for yourself. No one is coming to save you. In fact, no one but yourself can save you because it is you who you need saving from. If you're going to feel sorry for something, feel sorry for the time you have wasted in self-pity for the sake of self-pity, for the time you have wasted complaining that life is unfair, for the opportunities you have missed to grow because you let yourself be blinded by the sorrow of what could have been or isn't.

Tears were efficient when you were a baby that had no way to fend for yourself. They alerted those around you of your distress and allowed you to obtain things you could not acquire on your own. But you are not a baby. You are no longer a child. Your mother will not fix your problems, and tears, seen or unseen, external or internal, will not bring forth someone who can.

The problems you now face are of the internal sort which can only truly be understood by you and, therefore, can only be conquered by you—but first you must work to understand them. So wipe away your tears and work to find a resolution. You have the tools to handle any challenge, but how can you expect to use them if your vision is distracted by tears of regret and pity? You waste your focus on what isn't and fail to see what is. You wallow in alcohol and drugs as if they were a cure to your condition, despite knowing they're not.

Cry all you want, sulk in self-pity, and waste your time getting high or drunk to distract yourself from the hard truths of life, but know that whatever you do, this is your only life. You can live it with courage or cowardice; you can live it like a man or like a bitch.

LETTER II

You are not happy. Why? You blame your condition on not being born to good parents, not having the same privileges as another, or not having the money to live the lifestyle that you wish you had. You say you have suffered from adversity, from a terrible upbringing, from constant bad luck—it is always something else, isn't it? It's never you.

I am not claiming that your life has been easy. Many things have happened to you in which you had no choice in. You have experienced things that would make the strongest of men shudder had they been in your position. Scars riddle your body and serve as evidence that you are no stranger to pain. Yet, the scars that cannot be seen haunt you the most. Your heart has been broken many times, your trust in life and love shattered more than once.

But, when it comes to finding happiness, what does any of this mean — nothing.

No matter how tragic life is, the thing that stops one from finding happiness and peace is the same as it is for the person who has suffered minimal adversity — one's self. Beyond understanding yourself, it matters little how you arrived where you're at once you're there. What matters is what you do and how you act now that you are there.

For example, imagine you have been kidnapped, driven to the middle of nowhere, and left stranded; it matters how you arrived in terms of understanding how you can find your way back, but wasting your time blaming the people who took you there does nothing to save you. The only thing that will save you is yourself and how you decide to carry yourself. Will you adapt and build a new life at this location? Will you find within yourself the strength and persistence to make the trek back home or to a new location of your choosing? Or will you roll into a ball and cry, destining you to live a life determined by everything but yourself?

LETTER III

You traveled all this way in hopes of a life of adventure. You left home, family, and friends with the intent of finding meaning and purpose. You want to mimic that which you read in books and see in movies. But it was not here, at least not in the way you had imagined. You have tricked yourself into believing that a life of meaning is hidden somewhere far and unseen and that a life of purpose requires constant adventure. You were blind to the fact that even the greatest adventures consist of long periods of unrest and a succession of dull moments that last just as long. You were naive to the truth that many adventurers never experience happiness, peace, or purpose.

LETTER IV

You wish others were better, more faithful, more kind. You fear that you may never find anyone you can be fully committed to because it's impossible to find someone who will be fully committed to you. You are convinced that a person with such loyalty doesn't exist, that given enough time and the right situation, they will let you down. But, if you consider yourself a person with such loyalty, how can you say they don't exist? If you are able to live to such standards, then be sure that others can too. So make sure you live by the principles you value so much. The only way you can feel safe trusting others with your heart is if you can trust yourself with their heart. You can't expect others to live to standards that you fail to reach. Be the change you want to see.

LETTER V

Life is not a movie, but you expect it to be like one and often become frustrated when it is not. It shows in your spirit. It shows during the mundane moments of your life when you become disappointed over boredom. You are not able to enjoy the quiet parts of life and instead anxiously look for purpose in the form of material possessions, parties, adventures, romance, drugs, money, and sex—but who told you these things would bring you purpose or true happiness? None of these things are sustainable ways of living, and none make up an entire life, let alone a good life.

Don't be fooled by movies, stories, and books—life is not one thing. It is not one-dimensional. Life is not one romance followed by a "happily ever after" or one adventure followed by eternal satisfaction. Life is a mix of struggle, success, failure, happiness, sadness, depression, love, hate, adventure, and mundaneness—accept this truth, do not fight it. Learn to live life well in all its forms. Do not waste any more of your time in spite.

LETTER VI

You are not the main character. All eyes are not on you. People do not spend their time thinking about the embarrassing mistakes you have made. That is a fantasy in your head, a nightmare. It is why you take things so personally. You believe that the person who cut you off in traffic did so to piss you off, that the man taking too long to cross the street wants to make you late, and that every snicker you hear is directed at you or about you. How important you must think you are and how exhausting your life is because of it.

LETTER VII

Purpose in life. You have no purpose in life. Or maybe your purpose in life is whatever you decide it to be, or your purpose in life is to live it. I'm still unsure.

LETTER VIII

You are owed nothing. You must work for what you want. It will be hard. In some cases, you will give it your all and still fail. That's life. Don't resent it; live it.

LETTER IX

Your feelings are valid, but they are not facts. They are true to how you feel, but they are not objective. It may feel good to let them take over when you feel angry or annoyed, but they do not provide a clear understanding of any given situation. Don't be overcome by your emotions. Whenever a strong feeling arises, do not let it act on you. Take a moment to recognize it so that you do not act impulsively.

LETTER X

You have never tried your hardest at anything. You tried, but not with everything you had. You were too afraid of that kind of failure, the failure of someone that gave everything, every minute of his time, every drop of sweat, every drop of blood and ounce of effort to a goal, but despite all of it, failed. But do you not see? You *have* failed, and in the worst possible way—instead of giving everything you had, you lost everything you were given. Each opportunity purposely missed because you did not try. But it is not too late. You can still succeed in the goal of giving it your all, whatever it may be. In fact, let everything you do be worth the price of giving it your all, or don't do it. Do not let your goal be to win. Instead, let your goal be to give your all to whatever you find important.

LETTER XI

It's all your fault, all of it. It's not your fault, any of it. It doesn't matter, most of it. It matters most, all of it. Anyone of these is true if you want it to be. You are your thoughts. As you think, so you shall become, and so you will believe.

LETTER XII

You are too angry, too annoyed. Why do you make your life so difficult? Why are you so weak of mind that you let any slight disturbance set you off? You allow your mind to be conquered by anyone who happens to rub you the wrong way. You are quick to anger, quick to confrontation. Do you think being quick to anger makes you a man; do you think that hunting for confrontation makes you tough? Do you think you are solving the issue at hand by getting so flustered? Do you think you are proving something? All you are proving is that you are anyone's bitch. Controlled at the drop of a hat.

LETTER XIII

You wish to be normal. There is no normal. Everyone is weird in their own way. Besides, why are you so focused on how others see you? It doesn't matter how others perceive you when you are sure of yourself and your actions. If every action you make is backed by good intention and good reason, then why be concerned how anyone will see you?

LETTER XIV

You complain for nothing. You act as though the world is against you, as if every failure was not just a failure but an attack on you by nature, by man, and by god. Little do you know that you are not that important. The world does not stop for you; it does not take you into account when making any decision. The sun will not rise because you are cold, nor will it set because you are hot. The sun will rise and set in the places that nature has deemed necessary, and the same is true for your life. Your failures are no grand scheme against you. Nature's actions are not personal. The world is not attacking you. God has not left you, nor has he aimed to hurt you. God, mother nature, the divine universe— whatever you may call it— has set you on this earth as a part of nature, not separate from it.

LETTER XV

You are the cause of all your troubles. You are the answer to all your troubles. You can be content, and you can be free, but you must conquer yourself. You must come to an understanding with yourself on what it is that is truly worth worrying about and living for. You have wasted too much time on unimportant things. Stop and examine your life. Make a plan. Do something.

LETTER XVI

Aren't you tired of being sarcastic? Not everything in life requires a joke. Not every conversation requires a smart-ass comment. There is benefit in being serious, in being "real." But you hide, putting distance between you and real, filling the gap with an unending supply of humor and audacity.

LETTER XVII

Oh, how much time you have wasted wishing you were older, wishing you were younger. How much time you have spent fantasizing about a life you never lived, dreaming about the life you should have lived-- you completely miss the life you are living.

You wish you could go back in time to appreciate the good times with more enthusiasm and take advantage of the opportunities you missed due to fear or because you were shortsighted. Unfortunately, that is impossible. The moments of life you so fondly miss were not fully appreciated, opportunities were overlooked—a smarter you would take this as a lesson. They would understand that right now, at this very minute, you are living a period of your life that you will one day wish you could return to, to either appreciate it more or to take advantage of the countless opportunities you are missing because you are distracted. You are too concerned with what wasn't, what isn't, and what might not be. Just focus on what is. Live your days as if you were an 80-year-old version of yourself who has traveled back in time to live one more day as his former self, to live one more day in his old house, among his friends and family that he has lost once already. To appreciate the scenery, the sun, the stars, and the earth as someone who got the chance to relive life and is determined not to let any of it go to waste again.

LETTER XVIII

You think your job title is so important. You think your career and the heights you strive to reach are what really makes life worth living— you are wrong. You have no idea what it is in life that should be appreciated. You've never given it independent thought. Instead, you have followed along with whatever you were taught. You have been led to believe that status and success breed happiness, that you must commit a third of your life to work for someone in hopes of making enough money under a fancy enough title, that you can finally feel proud of yourself for having "made it" in life. However, status and reputation mean very little in the grand scheme of life. If, amid the peak of your career, you should be diagnosed with cancer and given months to live, watch how fast you discover what's really important; watch how fast you quit your job in order to focus on what's really important in life; watch how quickly you take back the 40 to 80 hours a week you once dedicated to a job you didn't even like. You were only in it to make money in order to live a life that you felt you deserved. You eventually had the money but no time; you could buy the things you desired but had no time to use them; you could afford that apartment you wanted but were too busy at work to enjoy it. But now you really don't have the time—it's no longer a choice. Death has come, and it waits for no one.

Do not wait for cancer to strike your body before you decide to live your life for yourself. For though you do not have cancer, there is a limit circumscribed to your time—it could be today, tomorrow, next week, or next year. So live as if you are dying, because you *are* dying, everyone is dying. We are not immortal, yet we live as though we are, putting important things off as if we have all the time in the world—a foolish mistake.

LETTER XIX

Stop talking over people. Let them finish what they have to say. Do yourself a favor and just shut up until you are sure that the other person is done talking. Create a space where both of you can be heard and understood—no matter the subject, no matter the person.

LETTER XX

You will one day die. Everyone you know will die. Everyone to have ever known you will die, and everyone who knew them will die too. Everything, as you know it, will one day cease to exist. This life you live, this existence, is a speck on the timeline of the universe. So what kind of glory are you searching for? Why do you wish for your name to be remembered for the ages when the ages themselves will one day not be remembered? Why not spend your time working to know yourself instead of worrying about whether strangers will know your name?

LETTER XXI

You say you want to carry yourself as a man, yet you let your emotions get the best of you. They hold on to you as one does with the reigns of a horse, steering it in a direction that the horse has no say in. And just as some horses, when unfairly treated, are pushed to exhaustion and even death, emotions, too, especially anger and depression, will work a man to death— death of reason, death of friendships, of romance, and death of one's self.

Do you think that your emotions are justified? Do you think they are facts? Do you think that just because you feel a certain type of way that it must be true? No, you're not so stupid to think that the world revolves around you, are you? You don't actually believe that the people you find annoying are trying to annoy you on purpose or that those you find offensive are trying to offend you? You say no, but you become defensive when someone does something that you think is wrong, and you become defensive when you feel attacked, despite not truly knowing the motives of the person speaking to you. That doesn't stop you from responding as though you have been attacked. That doesn't stop you from letting that fire in your gut fester to the point where you become annoyed, and it doesn't stop you from letting that annoyance spread throughout your body and become anger.

If you want to conquer yourself, you must first get your mind in order. You must be able to feel an emotion and yet not act on it. You must examine your emotions and study them so that you can overcome them and remain reasonable during difficult times—because though emotion is a beautiful part of humanity, it can tear down the strongest of men if left unexamined, ignored, and acted upon impulsively.

LETTER XXII

If you're going to change, you need to change today. Stop putting it off. It does not get easier. You know this because you have failed to put plan into action before, and you are the result of that failure. You cannot rely on your future self to solve your problems. You don't get to a certain age and magically receive the answers for your issues. It takes years of development to overcome one's self. Start now.

LETTER XXIII

Wake up. There is no finish line to living a good life. It is not something you obtain but something you sustain.

You say that you are not satisfied in life. You blame your lack of satisfaction on your shitty living situation, you blame it on your shitty job, and you blame it on your shitty car. You convince yourself that you could find satisfaction if you could only get a better job or obtain a higher position at your current job. So you invest all your time into work, and eventually, years later, you get that promotion, and with it comes all the things money can buy. Now you can finally be happy, for you should feel complete—you have the money, the apartment, and the nice car, yet the void is still there. Something still is not quite right.

You tell yourself that the real cause of your anxieties and sorrow must be from not owning a home. You work even harder, spending more time at the office. When you're not at work, you think about work. Your work becomes your life, but it pays off. You get another promotion and use the pay raise to buy a house. You're excited, but once things settle down, you realize you can still feel that void. From the outside perspective, you are a model of success. Everyone you meet sees that you have it all together. Yet, you still do not feel complete. Do you know why? Because you have spent all this time looking outside yourself for approval. You base your success on the opinions of others and spend all your time working to obtain things that you have been told are important. Discover for yourself what is important. Stop basing your definition of success on what you hear from other people, people who are living life for the first time, just like you. Examine their claim. Examine yourself.

LETTER XXIV

Everyone inherits problems from their parents. Parents are people, and people don't automatically become perfect when they have children—problems don't go away on their own they are passed down. But once you discover that your parents are to blame for your issues, it is no longer their fault if those problems continue unhindered. From that point on, it is on you—it's up to you to fix those issues, it's up to you to not let those issues control your life, it's up to you to grow.

Imagine you bought a used car that turned out to have bad brakes and, after discovering the issue, continued to drive the vehicle. You would be at fault for any damage your car caused to others or yourself, and rightfully so. You knew there was an issue, yet you did nothing to fix it. Instead, you decided to drive the car while cursing the one who sold it to you, as if you could blame the hurt you might cause on that person, even though you were fully aware of the issue. It's the same in life: trauma caused by your upbringing isn't a get-out-of-jail-free card to act however you want.

If you find that your parents are to blame for any issue you might have picked up during childhood, there is no benefit in blaming them for your current mistakes or failings. Once you identify the root cause, it is up to you to fix it. That doesn't mean that you didn't have it tough, it doesn't mean that your upbringing wasn't unfair, and it doesn't mean that your parents were right in the way they acted or in the way they treated you. But blame only does so much. If your aim in life is to seethe at the thought of how unfairly you have been treated, then go ahead and blame. But, if your aim is to grow, overcome, and conquer yourself, then use blame only to identify the root cause of your issue so that you may better understand what you need to beat it.

LETTER XXV

You don't have to comment on every issue. Sometimes you can just listen to someone you disagree with without voicing your opinion. Not everything needs your input. Not everyone wants your input. And it's ok to admit that you know nothing about a subject, rather than try to piece together a position based on the limited information you have.

LETTER XXVI

Why do you battle over every disagreement you encounter with those you love? Stop creating unnecessary division. Not everything requires a rebuttal, and not every conversation requires you to "win." Is your ego so fragile that you must be right about everything? Look deep inside yourself—why do you feel this need to prove yourself? What does it stem from? Are you so insecure that to be seen as "wrong" is such a terrible thing that you would risk losing your sanity? Ask yourself whether you would rather be right or happy.

LETTER XXVII

You will never love anyone the way you want if you do not first love yourself. To love yourself is the first step toward being able to love someone the way that you want to be loved and the way that they should be loved.

LETTER XXVIII

Stop complaining about what you do not have or did not achieve. Either do something about it or shut the fuck up. You either work to change it or work to accept it. If you want to live a healthy life, at times, the only option you will have is to accept it. Otherwise, you will end up living in a personal hell.

You should know that everyone pays their dues. Everyone misses out on something in pursuit of something else. The rich man gives up his time for wealth, while the family man gives up his time and wealth for family. The rich man may not regret his decision until he is old and lonely, whereas the family man may not realize how lucky he is until he is old and loved. Both have won and lost in their own way. Stop complaining about what you do not have and become content with your reasons for not having them.

Every decision is made with some degree of intention. Your problem is that you deny that your actions are responsible for your current situation and state of mind. Every decision you have made was made with intention. Do not say they weren't just because you did not pause long enough to examine the intention of your actions.

There was a period in life where the intention of each decision you made was to feel as least uncomfortable as possible. Your life reflects that, yet you're upset because you now want the life of someone who made decisions with the intent to grow, no matter how uncomfortable they might feel in the moment. It is too late. You do not have that life--and if you continue on the same path, you never will.

LETTER XXIX

Do not bail when life gets uncomfortable. Do not be so weak that you can't stand sustained moments of discomfort. You talk a big game from the sidelines, but when the moment comes to put your words into action, to actually be the person you claim to be—that you want to be—you fail. You let that nauseous feeling in your gut lead you away from the feeling in your heart.

LETTER XXX

If you're going to do something, own it. Do not be concerned with how others will view you. If you're not right to do this thing, then don't do it at all. But, if after deliberation and thought on the subject, you think it is something worthy of doing, then who cares how others will view you? There is no need to hide who you are or what you like for the sake of someone else. When you censor or change yourself so that you may "fit in" for the sake of fitting in, you are doing yourself a disservice. You deny yourself *yourself*.

LETTER XXXI

You're better sober.

LETTER XXXII

You are you. No one is coming to replace you with the person you think you should be, and no one can replace your former self with the person you think you should have been. Every mistake, error, awkward moment, and embarrassing action that you made in the past is a part of you. Don't run from it, own it. To run from it is to run from yourself; to hate it is to hate a part of yourself. You don't have to like who you were or how you acted in the past, and it may be true that the person you are today would not want anything to do with the person you used to be. However, you must come to terms with the fact that you would never be who you are today if it wasn't for the growth you achieved as a direct result of the mistakes you made.

You need to understand that your former self is not you, or it is you to the extent that a cake is an egg—yes, a cake contains eggs, but a cake is not an egg; it tastes nothing like an egg, smells nothing like an egg, looks nothing like an egg, and feels nothing like an egg. However, without the egg, the cake isn't much of a cake. It doesn't hold together as well, the texture is poor, and it doesn't taste as good. You can not like eggs and, at the same time, appreciate them for their role in making a good cake. Again, it's the same in life--appreciate the mistakes you've made for the lessons they have brought.

Do not waste your time obsessing over past mistakes or glorifying them, but when they come up in thought, own them. Own them in the same way you would own the mistakes you made as a baby. No one cares or is riddled with anxiety because they shit themselves as a baby or cried over silly things as a kid. People are more forgiving because these things are expected of a child. But mistakes and growth should be expected at all ages—it doesn't stop at childhood. Growth isn't achieved in a day or in just one period of your life. It is a continuous process and different for everyone. So you must be just as understanding of your more recent failings as you are of your failings as an infant. Learn from them.

LETTER XXXIII

You are lazy. Lazy, not relative to the average person, but lazy relative to the person you need to become to achieve what you want. Here is the biggest issue—you are a good actor. Such a good actor that you have convinced yourself that your time is not being wasted. Unfortunately, for you, the results do not lie. What will you do? Remain the same or take action? MOVE! What do you wait for? Failure is better than no attempt. Finish what you fucking started. Stop making goals and start completing them.

LETTER XXXIV

You cannot control anyone but yourself. Stop trying to take charge of the feelings and opinions of other people. Realize that in this life, in the form that we live, and on the level we exist, we are only able to control ourselves. Similarly, we can only truly understand ourselves, meaning that most people will never fully understand you in the same way that you understand yourself. But do not hold that against them. They cannot be held accountable for not being able to understand you. They have not viewed every minute of your life as you have. They have not lived through your eyes or experiences. But it is the same in reverse, which is why you must not be quick to judge or quick to trust.

LETTER XXXV

Brainwashed. You have been brainwashed and you haven't the slightest idea of it. You believe that happiness is something you can reach from a single achievement, or multiple achievements:

"If only I had money,"

"If only I had that job,"

"If only I knew what job I want to have,"

"If only I had someone to love… then I would be happy, then I could rid myself of this depression."

These things will not lead you to happiness. Happiness is not a thing that you own once you obtain it. It is a fleeting state of being that leaves almost as quick as it arrives. A succession of achievements will not make you feel whole. You must not make happiness your goal. You should live life in such a way that you never even think about wanting to be happy.

LETTER XXXVI

Everybody that lives is going to die. This is a fact of nature. Your greatest friends and closest family will all die. It doesn't matter how much you love them. Death does not discriminate by love, age, or generosity. It waits for no one. The only thing you can do about it is to appreciate those around you while they are here. Appreciate them from the perspective of someone that has already lost them once.

LETTER XXXVII

You are not important, and that's ok. No one is important. Or, at least, no one is important unless someone decides they are, and even at that, they are only important to that person. It's like the concept of "cool." Everyone is cool to someone, but that same person to someone else is lame. But you shouldn't let your concept of "cool" be guided by someone else. It only has to be "cool" to you. The same goes for "important." In most cases, no one needs to think that what you're doing or what you're striving for is important—no one but you, that is. Remember this next time you feel self-conscious. Who the fuck is anyone else to dictate what's important to you or what you find joy in? To let them have jurisdiction over your feelings is like letting them tell you what kind of food you like or what type of music you enjoy.

LETTER XXXVIII

People don't have dreams, they make them. Stop complaining that you don't have a purpose and make one.

LETTER XXXIX

You fucked up. It happened. You said something stupid or did something stupid, and now you feel a deep embarrassment, a strong regret. But dwelling on these feelings do nothing to fix the problem. They only introduce you to the problem. Once introduced to the issue, embarrassment and regret become useless, a waste of time and energy. Learn from it and there is no reason to feel anxious about it.

LETTER XL

You need to calm down. Take a step back and reflect on the situation. What are you looking to gain from this conversation?

Book II

Things to Understand

LETTER XLI

There is very little in this world that you can control. Do not let that discourage you. Use it to your advantage. There is freedom in understanding what you can and cannot control. When you know what you can control, you know what is worth caring about; when you understand what you cannot control, you know what not to spend your time worrying about. Those who understand this have more time to enjoy life and indulge in the areas they have control. But, those who do not understand spend their time fighting for control over things that can never be theirs. They agonize over the thoughts of others; they worry about events they have no power over and are overcome with anxiety at random hours with no understanding as to why.

LETTER XLII

Life is not easy. Do not trick yourself into believing that the hardship you face is a product of you. Struggle is a natural part of living, but you are not your struggle. You are your reaction to the struggle. Your failures do not have to define you. However, if you believe that they do, they will. We are the creators of our problems. Man decides what he takes issue with. If this was not the case, all humans would find suffering and joy in the same things. But we don't. Instead, what angers one man delights another. What brings tears to one person brings joy to another. Decide today to stop seeing struggle and hardship as misfortune. See it as an opportunity for growth. Never fear it; welcome it.

LETTER XLIII

It is possible to make it out of your current state of mind, despite what you might think. All it takes to change your life is one decision to be the best version of yourself. But, the trick is, you must make this decision every day. You will fuck up, accept it. But when you fall, you pick yourself back up, you crawl if you have to, but never stop moving. Each day you must move towards bettering yourself. Understand that you will never change your life until you change something you do daily.

LETTER XLIV

Become comfortable with simply existing; to be in the present moment without any specific purpose. See the beauty of life without distraction. Mastering this will give you more enjoyment than any song, movie, or book ever could. You will never be bored in idle moments and never feel anxious for distraction.

LETTER XLV

What do you want? Who do you want to be? You don't know, and that's fine. For now, let your goal be to be the best version of yourself. When you struggle to find motivation in your everyday life, whether that comes in the form of a struggle to get out of bed or a struggle to get out of your head, stop and think to yourself— "What would the best version of me do? What decision would I make right now if I was the person I wanted to be?" And then do that thing, even if you don't want to. It's as easy as that and as hard as that. You could be the best version of yourself today, right now! You just need to commit. Once you start to work on yourself, the rest will follow. Everything will fall into place when you start living life for yourself.

LETTER XLVI

There is a way out of the depression that you feel. All is not hopeless. You will make it out, but you and your soul must keep moving forward. If you can't run, you walk. If you can't walk, crawl. For now, the rate at which you move does not matter. A mile, a foot, an inch—whatever, just move. How do you expect to crawl out of this rut you are in if you don't keep moving?

Do not give up. Keep moving.

LETTER XLVII

Be careful not to waste your thoughts. Every unintentional thought is a wasted thought, a missed opportunity to improve yourself. The more intention you place behind your thoughts, the more growth you will achieve in the area you focus on. So direct your thoughts towards a purpose. If you don't know what that purpose is yet, let finding that purpose be the purpose. The mind is like a garden; tend to it properly, and you can grow whatever you want. But leave it unattended, and it will bring forth things you had no say in. Weeds will take over the plot, and seeds from nearby plants will sprout and grow to unimaginable sizes. Whether neglected or cared for, your garden will bring forth.

LETTER XLVIII

Your reality is what you decide it is. How you look at things in life will be how they exist to you. If you decide something is good, it will be good; if you decide it is bad, it will be bad; if you believe something is scary, it will be scary; if you think you are unlucky, you will be unlucky. You carry around the weight of whatever it is you believe—you are the sum of your thoughts.

LETTER XLIX

When it comes to keeping promises you make to yourself, think less. Do not talk yourself out of commitments that you have made to yourself. If you say you're getting up at 5 A.M. tomorrow morning, as soon as that alarm goes off, get out of bed. Do not give yourself time to rationalize your way out of the situation. Every promise to yourself must be like giving and taking a command. You command yourself to get up and, like a good soldier, you carry out the command without question.

LETTER L

Everything works out. It always does. Where ever your life takes you, it will be the right path (if you want it to be). Every mistake you have made was necessary for you to be the person you are today. We only live one life. There is no "practice round," mistakes will be made. They have to be. No one is born all-knowing; no one is born perfect. So don't be so hard on yourself when you make a mistake, and don't stress over your past mistakes. The only thing you can do about your mistakes is learn from them. Some of your biggest mistakes will lead to your biggest wins, your most important growth, and your favorite moments. You just can't see it now.

LETTER LI

Life has made you into who you are—the good and the bad. You have made mistakes that you thought would destroy you and have felt pain that you thought would be eternal, but you didn't succumb to self-pity. Instead, you looked for lessons in tragedy; you fought to keep moving while depressed; you became observant of your blessings and merciful towards yourself. Life can feel bleak, but it doesn't have to—you will see that soon enough. You will one day love yourself. You will one day become a friend to yourself. It's going to be okay.

LETTER LII

It's okay to feel sad. Emotions are a natural part of being alive. In fact, you will be sad many more times in your life. You will also be happy many more times in your life.

LETTER LIII

You are not alone in your struggle. Others have passed through the same battles that you encounter now. It is possible to make it out. It is possible to resist the urge to quit; it's possible to silence the negative voices and lift up the positive ones. It is possible to love yourself.

LETTER LIV

There is no shame in being temporarily discouraged. You should be ashamed if you let that feeling of discouragement put out the fire within you. You should be ashamed if, when that fire goes out, you become okay with sitting in darkness. Keep your fire going.

LETTER LV

Do not look down on yourself for your mistakes; look down on yourself for not learning from them. You were not born perfect, so don't expect to be. If you want to grow, you will have to make mistakes—dumb mistakes, silly mistakes, brave mistakes, cowardly mistakes. Mistakes are the means by which you will master life, *if* you learn from them.

LETTER LVI

This life that you are living is the only one you have. Do not waste it crying over a life that doesn't exist. You are frustrated that you are not the person you thought you would be at this age. You look at your life and have none of the things you thought you would. You waste your time on such thoughts. Why are you living in another world? You cry for a life that does not exist. You waste the present sulking over a memory of a dream. But when you die, this will be the only life you lose, not your made-up fairytale. So live for today, live in today. Let today be the dream that you want to live.

LETTER LVII

Everyone is wrong in someone's opinion. So just care about your own. But let your opinion be one based on reason and common sense. Hold it to the same scrutiny that you would hold the opinion of others to. Otherwise, why have confidence in your opinion? If you think it is too much of a hassle to question and research a specific opinion, then keep that opinion to yourself. Many people have no idea where their opinions come from but are still willing to preach them. They are unaware of how they were formed because they've never questioned it. A foolish mistake because our opinions inevitably become our life. They are the lens through which we see the world through. Become aware of how important they are.

LETTER LVIII

You feel like you have failed in life. You have failed to do what is expected of you, or at least what you think is expected of you. On the outside, you look calm and collected, but there is a fire inside you. One that burns hot. You hate who you think you are, you hate your life, or at least you say you do. But the truth is, you are in the depths of discovery. These trials will lead you to great things. The pain you feel now is necessary. It is the fertilizer for growth.

LETTER LIX

Never let your emotions get the best of you. It makes you weak. The man who is quick to lash out is slow to think. He gives up control of his mind to anger, fear, and seduction. Take a moment and breathe. Acknowledge your feelings, then asses the situation with a clear mind.

Not letting your emotions get the best of you doesn't mean you can't experience joy, anger, happiness, frustration, or any other feeling that comes with being human. It means not acting solely on emotion.

LETTER LX

You are struggling to find a purpose. For now, let your purpose be to improve yourself. Improve yourself physically, mentally, spiritually, or any other way you can think of. Everything else will fall into place.

The best thing you can do for yourself is to better yourself. It will take time and dedication. There is no set road map to life. You must make your own, one day at a time. You must learn as you go. At times it will feel hopeless, and at other times confusing. Keep to the task. Improve yourself, and you will improve your life.

LETTER LXI

Don't act out when feeling triggered or worked up. Instead, see it as an opportunity to test your self-control, patience, and composure. You are weak when you let situations get the best of you and erupt in anger or fester in annoyance. What good does it do to let yourself become worked up over any unfortunate or triggering event? It solves nothing. All it proves is that you have no control over yourself, just like a child. It gives you nothing but takes from you the most valuable thing you have—time. It then wastes that time, keeping you in a state of frustration long after the event has occurred.

LETTER LXII

Discipline is everything. If you want to master life, you must master discipline. You must conquer yourself. You must silence the lazy you, the weak you, the unsure you. Everyone knows what they need to do, but few do it. Not because they don't have the power to, but because they do not have the discipline, the commitment, the love for self. Love yourself, commit to yourself. Start with small tasks and work your way up from there.

LETTER LXIII

It doesn't matter if you fail; expect it. Life is not all rainbows and butterflies. There is struggle in this world. There is pain, anger, poverty, and failure. But you are not any of these. You are resilient, driven, and determined. You have the tools to overcome any obstacle. When you fall, get back up, and don't bitch about falling; learn from it.

LETTER LXIV

Be skeptical of appearances. Do not let them fool you. Your first impression of things is not always correct. Being beautiful doesn't make a person good-hearted, being cute doesn't make a dog friendly, being religious doesn't make a person trustworthy, being poor doesn't make a person unfulfilled, and being rich doesn't make a person feel whole.

LETTER LXV

No matter the situation, you can benefit. Do not look at any outcome as a loss; do not look at any event as bad. Change your mindset. There is a lesson to be learned from every loss. There is something to be gained from every failure. How can something be terrible if it leads to something good? How can you label an event a failure if you walked away a better person? There is a win in every unfavorable event. Focus on this instead since it is within your power to control, whereas the event itself is set in stone and out of your reach.

Book III

Miscellaneous

Scribbles from my former self

I

The old man replied:

"As you are, I once was. As I am, you will one day be."

Time does not stop. It creeps by steadily, almost unnoticed, until it is impossible not to notice it.

II

My soul isn't of so little value that I would exchange it for money. I would not dedicate my life to working a job I disdain just to have a title to show off or money to spend aimlessly. People have convinced themselves that this is the only way to live a life they can be proud of. They dedicate their energy, time, and heart to working for a company they share nothing of importance with. They wake up every day, argue themselves out of bed, and begrudgingly get ready for a job that they try to find any excuse to skip out on. After dragging themselves through their shift, they come home, distract themselves for a few hours, and do it all over again the next day. These same people seem confused when feelings of depression take over. "I don't know why I feel this way," one might say, but how could you not know? You have dedicated your soul to something which has no value to you. You are taking the most valuable thing you have, time, and offering it as sacrifice so that you can make enough money to buy the things you think will fulfill you. You are convinced that there is no other way to live life. That you must work a job you don't like to have the life you want, though you may never be able to enjoy it,

Of course, many have no option but to work such jobs. They have children to provide for or other family to care for. In this case, it is not the job they dedicate their life to but their children-- a noble pursuit.

III

There is risk in love. There is risk in all great things.

IV

If life had a roadmap or a list of directions, would I follow it? I wonder what it would look like. Would it give specific ages for specific life events: "Must have first job by age 16," "Should be married by age 30," "Retire by age 65." Or would it just say, "Live but do not impede on the life of others without permission?"

V

Our traditions, thoughts, and feelings are influenced by our upbringing and geological location. What's important to one group of people may not be important to another. The Sacred traditions of one tribe may come off as a comedy routine to another. Good food in one country is disgusting in another. I think it's this matter of relativity that makes life so confusing, yet that same relativity makes it so simple. The choice is yours.

VI

"The grass is always greener on the other side." No, the grass is only greener where you water it.

VII

You're a fool to trust everyone and just as big of a fool to trust no one.

VIII

Learn to be decisive.

IX

You said you were different, you said you were better, but it's another day and it's the same damn weather.

X

I feel desperate. I feel late. I feel like a failure. But what rubric am I basing that on? Love, money, worldly success, the opinions of others, my perceived opinion of the opinion of others? The pointlessness of life, the endless drifting, the idea that if everything went right, it would still feel wrong. I long for a movie-like life. Despite the intensity of these emotions, I know they're bullshit. I know the opinions of others have no place in how I decide to value myself. Maybe it's my opinion of self that needs to be shifted. I need to take action.

XI

Trust is the firm belief in the reliability, truth and strength of another person.

XII

Accept it. Don't be controlled by lingering emotions. Be logical where logic doesn't exist. You are where you are because of you. If you don't like it, change it. If you do, continue to work on it.

XIII

I drank all the gin and ate all the Digiorno.

XIV

The life you live is the only life you lose.

XV

Live today in such a way that you would be comfortable with dying tomorrow.

XVI

Let every move be intentional.

XVII

You are not one event.

XVIII

Accept humbly, let go easily.

XIX

Don't neglect reading. The right book can change your life. Some people devote their entire life to a subject and write extensively on it; what took them nearly their whole life to learn, you can learn in a few days. But don't be foolish to believe that because something is in a book it must be true. It is always important to do your due diligence.

.

XX

Fear is a liar.

XXI

Another day in paradise. Let's go.

Made in the USA
Las Vegas, NV
17 November 2024

11979048R00069